WHAT HAPPENS WHEN I'M SCARED

A GUIDE TO TRICKY FEELINGS AND BIG EMOTIONS

BY CLAUDIA HERMAN

ILLUSTRATED BY
JOHN PETER MEIRING

For more information you can find me here:

📞 07966556094

✉ claudiahermantherapies@outlook.com

f @Claudia Herman Therapeutic Support

🌐 claudiahermantherapeuticsupport.com

What Happens When I'm Scared

Written by Claudia Herman
Illustrated by John Peter Meiring

Copyright 2021 Claudia Herman
First Published 2021
All Rights Reserved.

ISBN: 978-1-8384215-0-2

The rights of the author and illustrator have been asserted in accordance with Sections 77 and 78 of the Copyright Designs and Patents Act, 1988.

TAUK Kids **Children's Book Publishers**
A Division of Team Author UK

If you are a young person reading this book, congratulations for your excellent choice of reading matter!

All of us, kids, grown-ups, teachers, parents, everyone, we all face challenges sometimes. It is really important to know that the challenges we face will not last forever. When we face challenges it's not our fault. Often, we blame ourselves for situations over which we have no control. This is how we make sense of the world — but it's not true. When we're having a tricky time or struggling with big or tricky feelings it is really important that we are supported. Some jobs are too big for us to do on our own. I hope you have grown-ups and friends who care about you and are able to look after you. If you do not feel able to talk to your grown-ups or friends about a difficulty, there are still people who can help you.

childline.org.uk or phone 0800 1111
youngminds.org.uk or text 85258
talktofrank.com or phone 0300 123 6600 — this one is if you have worries or questions about drugs

I hope you enjoy the book and please get support when things are difficult. You deserve to be safe and looked after.

Much love, Claudia xx

Your brain and my brain — all brains, are really clever at keeping us safe.

WE ALL HAVE REALLY CLEVER BRAINS!

SURVIVA IS COOL

Humans have evolved over millions of years.

Human beings are all about survival.

YEAH MAN.

UGG!

PREFRONTAL CORTEX

HYPOTHALAMUS

HIPPOCAMPUS

BRAIN STEM

AMYGDALA

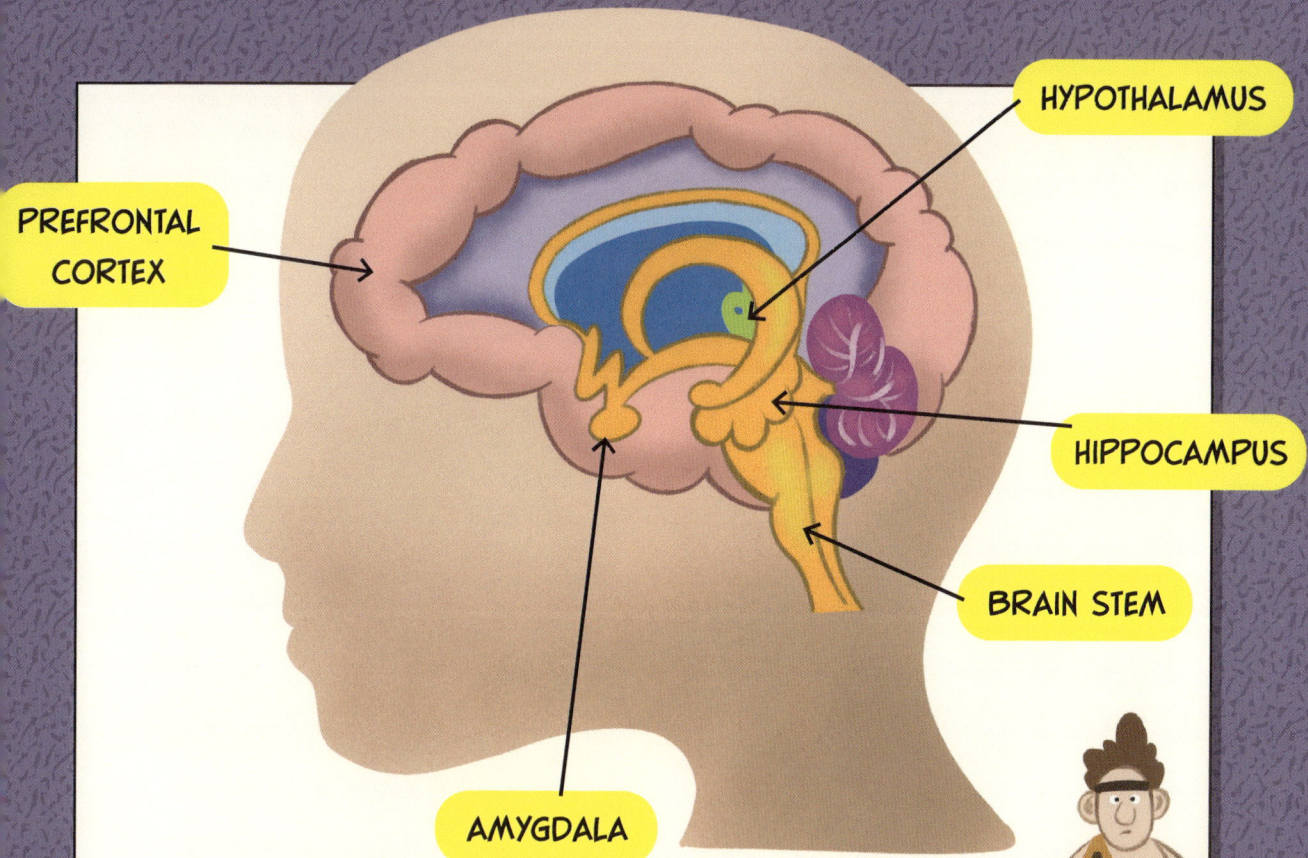

Our BRAIN STEM does all the super important stuff like reminding us to breathe.

Then, there is our AMYGDALA. This is our 'cave man' or our 'surviving' brain. This bit of brain is what stopped our cave man ancestors from getting eaten by sabre tooth tigers.

Most of us, today, do not need to worry about being eaten by sabre tooth tigers.

But our amygdala still works super hard to keep us safe!

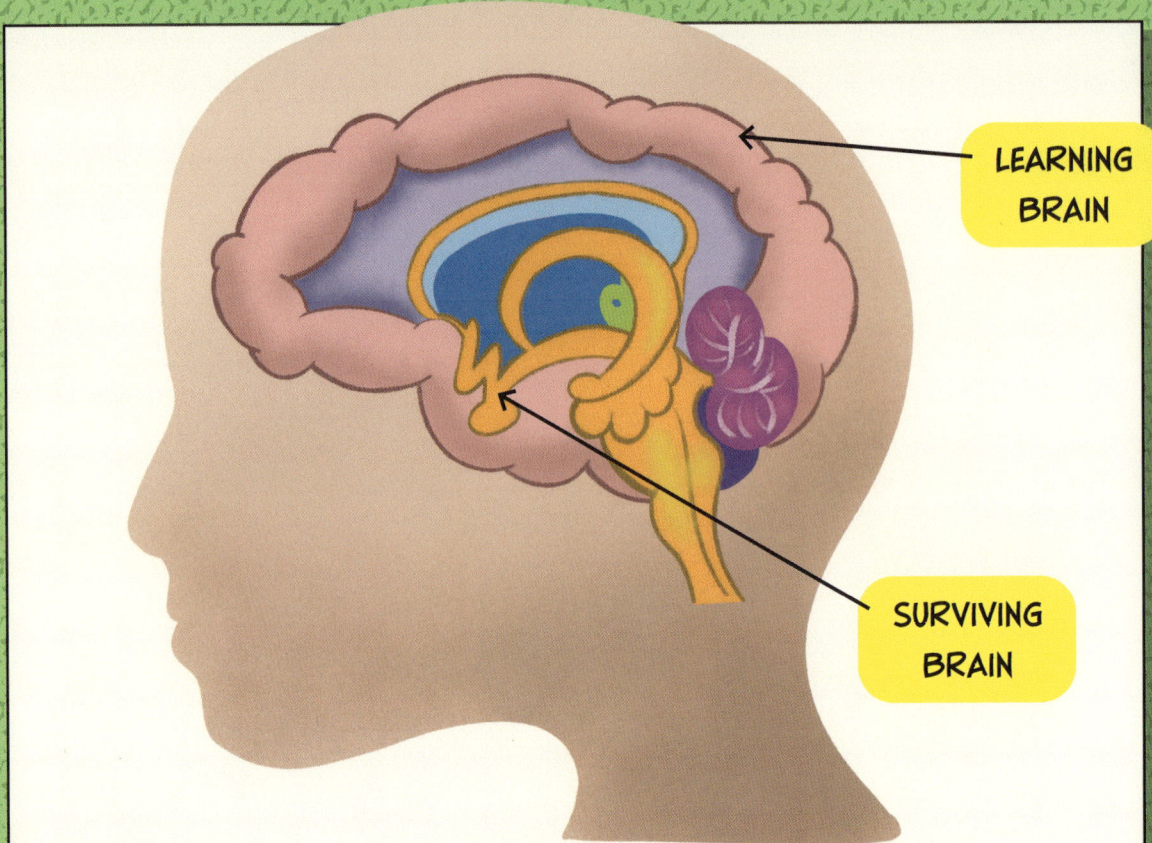

LEARNING BRAIN

SURVIVING BRAIN

On top of our amygdala is all the clever stuff. The 'LEARNING' or 'THINKING' brain.

When we are scared our 'thinking' brain goes off line and our 'CAVE MAN' or 'SURVIVING' brain — our *amygdala*, takes over.

AARGH!

I'M SCARED SO THAT MEANS MY SURVIVING BRAIN IS IN CHARGE! YIKES!

Our brain is essentially made up of upstairs people and downstairs people.

The downstairs people live in the amygdala. The people who live here are Angry Annie, Frightened Fred, Scared Sid and Worried Wilf. Your downstairs people might have different names.

ANGRY ANNIE

SCARED SID

FRIGHTENED FRED

WORRIED WILF

Angry Annie, Frightened Fred, Scared Sid and Worried Wilf are always looking out for us. They work hard to keep us safe. They never take a day off.

When Angry Annie, Frightened Fred, Scared Sid or Worried Wilf spot a problem they sound an alarm.

WE'VE GOT A PROBLEM!!

It's a lot like a fire alarm. It cannot tell whether your house is burning down and everyone is in terrible danger OR you just burnt your toast a bit.

OH NO!

ARGH!!

EVERYBODY PANIC!

When the downstairs people set off the fire alarm they cannot hear the upstairs people.

The upstairs people are Clever Clara, Kind Kevin, Good Choices Gertrude and Gentle Jen.

The upstairs people do all sorts of clever stuff. We need these people when we're at school.

ROAR!!

ARGH!

A SABRE TOOTH TIGER!!

QUICK! SOUND THE ALARM!

When the downstairs people get scared and worried that we might get eaten by a sabre tooth tiger they set off the fire alarm and no one can hear the upstairs people.

I'M SO SCARED!

HOW COULD THIS HAPPEN?!

I DON'T KNOW WHAT TO DO!

The upstairs people are really clever and have great ideas. But the downstairs people can't hear them.

THERE ARE LOADS OF WAYS TO DEAL WITH A SABRE TOOTH TIGER.

THE ALARM WILL HELP ...

... THERE'S NO WAY I CAN FIX THIS BY MYSELF!

When the downstairs people set off the fire alarm our body releases a powerful chemical called adrenalin. Adrenalin is super helpful if we need to fight or run away. It gives us energy and super human strength.

ADRENALIN POWERS, ASSEMBLE!

... ERR... IT SEEMS MY POWERS AREN'T REALLY NEEDED AFTER ALL.

If we don't need to fight or run away — because there is no sabre toothed tiger, no house fire, just a bit of burnt toast, there is nowhere for the adrenalin to go.

When we are full of adrenalin we feel shaky, jittery, wobbly.

I CAN'T STOP SHAKING!!

HELP! I CAN'T CONCENTRATE ON ANYTHING BECAUSE I'M TOO JITTERY!

Maybe our hands or knees shake.

MY TUMMY HURTS! OUCH!

Maybe we feel sick or have tummy pains.

It takes about forty minutes for our adrenalin levels to return back to normal — to how they were before we were scared.

WOW, SO LEMURS COME FROM MADAGASCAR...

I'M GOING TO DRAW SOME LEMURS IN ART LESSON

ARGH! I FEEL SO SHAKY. I CAN'T CONCENTRATE!

THAT'S AMAZING! LEMURS ARE REALLY COOL CREATURES!

Forty minutes is a long time. It's a whole lesson.

Things that might help to get rid of the adrenalin are:

* Rolling and kneading play doh

* Going for a run

* Doing some star jumps

* Bouncing on a trampoline

* Cuddling a pet or a grown-up who you trust

* Puffing out air as hard as you can

* Singing your favourite song really loud

* Dancing like a crazy person to your favourite song ...

... You can probably think of lots more!

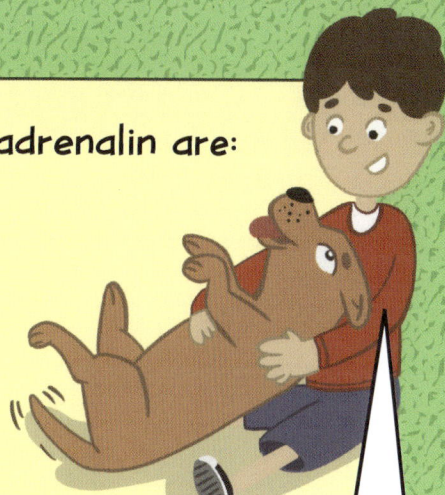

THIS FURRY GUY IS THE BEST!

THIS SONG IS SO COOL!

Working with a grown-up who you trust, you can start to think about your triggers if you feel like you want to. Your triggers are the things that make you feel scared. Often we don't understand why we feel scared.

It can be helpful to think about our past and things that have happened to us so that we can understand why we still feel scared now.

Eventually, our amygdala can learn to trust that we're safe and to recognise when it is only a bit of burnt toast.

Feeling scared and having lots of adrenaline can make us feel very tired. Feeling scared and tired makes learning and being at school really hard for us. It's not our fault.

HAVING SOME GOOD FRIENDS HELPS YOU TO SEE WHEN SOMETHING BAD IS JUST A BIT OF BURNT TOAST!

It is simply our brain working super hard — maybe a little too hard, to keep us safe.

YOU'VE GOT THIS!

Draw a picture of something that scares you.

TRY CHOOSING A PIECE OF MUSIC THAT IS ANGRY ...

... THEN CREATE DANCE MOVES TO GET THE ADRENALINE OUT!

Draw a picture or create a 3D model of something that makes you feel safe.

Guide Gentle Jen and Good Choices Gertrude through the maze to remind Angry Annie and Worried Wilf that burnt toast is ok.

START!

FINISH!

Can you work out which puzzle piece doesn't fit?

Using the key, colour in the picture to reveal a toothy surprise!

COLOUR KEY!
- ⭐ Orange
- 🔺 Brown
- 🟥 Red
- ⚪ Beige

A few words for the grown-ups

If you are an individual or an organisation wishing to move away from a 'behaviour management' model towards a 'trauma informed' model you have come to the right place. What do I mean by 'trauma'?

I use 'trauma' as a broad term. Why? Well, one person's 'mild inconvenience' can be another person's 'trauma' and vice versa. Trauma is not competitive and there is little to be gained from attempting to measure trauma — in my opinion.

Factors affecting our perception of trauma include our protective or resilience factors and ACEs — Adverse Childhood Experiences.

Why are ACEs such a big deal? Surely, babies and young children forget stuff that happens to them?

There are memories we are able to verbalise. There are also memories that are not stored away verbally — from when we were pre-verbal — we didn't have the words. They are stored emotionally. We might have smells, textures, places, foods that bring us comfort, anxiety or distress for reasons that we are not able to put into words.

As we mature and begin to appreciate the complexity of human existence, we realise it's not all about us.

For babies and young children, it is 'all about them'. So, when something bad, or something they perceive as being bad, happens to them the only explanation that makes any sense is that it is their fault. They're a bad person.

For example, a baby in special care or ICU can have no understanding that every time a medical professional carries out a procedure that is painful to them it is necessary in order to save their life. The only possible perception for the baby is that 'adults hurt me', 'I am bad'.

Young people who find themselves in the care system might feel it is their fault and that their experiences mean that they are a bad kid. Although we know this isn't true it is unimaginably painful for a young person.

Fast forward to parents who have lived through their own trauma of fearing for the survival of their very ill child. They might be incredibly grateful for the good outcome that was achieved whilst unable to shake the fear that they lived with during that time. Plus, this incredibly cherished child might be presenting with challenging behaviours as a consequence of their own fear and confusion resulting from their traumatic experience of being very unwell.

What if your experience of becoming a parent was traumatic? What if, for reasons outside of your control, your parenthood dream was (or is) more like a nightmare?

You're probably beginning to see just how complex human beings can be and how relatively common experiences can impact on our emotional well-being, sense of self and our relationships with those closest to us.

This is just one very small example.

Other perfectly 'normal' curve balls life tends to throw our way include, loss, bereavement, divorce, illness, life changes, neurodiversity, medical conditions.

It doesn't take much to wobble our sense of ourselves in the world and to wobble our attachments to others.

When our young people are finding things tough, it's not about us. When they show their struggles in ways that we find unacceptable, it still isn't about us. If we cannot 'fix' things for our young people, we are not failing them. We are all doing our best. We are all learning together. You've got this grown-ups!

ABOUT THE AUTHOR

I have over twenty years of supporting vulnerable children and families as a teacher, child protection officer, SENDCo and therapeutic foster carer, and I am a mum to two fabulous neurodiverse superstars. I cannot take any credit for this story without thanking my incredible family and friends — Emily, Tyler, Rohan, Bert, Joy, Sophie, Sioban, Sue Flint, Catherine Hews, Madge Foulkes — it really does take a village. This story really belongs to my kids. My son joined our family six and a half years ago. This story helped him to understand his challenges. He named all the upstairs and downstairs brain people. My daughter has been, and still is, key in facilitating his healing journey in ways she doesn't even know.

f @Claudia Herman Therapeutic Support

🌐 claudiahermantherapeuticsupport.com

✉ claudiahermantherapies@outlook.com

ABOUT THE ILLUSTRATOR

John Peter Meiring is an illustrator and animator who lives in London, England, surrounded by the Thames and lovely forests. After studying advertising design, he started doing drawings for companies and animating for the creative industries, until he found out that illustrating for children is such a wonderful field.
He prefers creating illustrations digitally on his graphic tablets, always trying to hide the pen from his crafty but adorable dog.

🌐 oddpumpkinstudio.com

📷 instagram.com/oddpumpkinstudio

Printed in Great Britain
by Amazon